MAR 2 7 2017

# Girls Play

Girls
JOIN THE
TEAM

# FIELD HOCKEY

David Anthony

PowerKiDS
press.

New York

Published in 2017 by The Rosen Publishing Group, Inc.
29 East 21st Street, New York, NY 10010

First Edition

Editor: Katie Kawa
Book Design: Tanya Dellaccio

Photo Credits: Cover Aspen Photo/Shutterstock.com; pp. 5, 22 Air Images/Shutterstock.com; p. 7 (bottom) https://commons.wikimedia.org/wiki/File:Relief_pentelic_marble_%22Ball_Players%22_510-500_BC,_NAMA_3476_102587.jpg; p. 7 (top) https://commons.wikimedia.org/wiki/File:Constance_Applebee_circa_1903.jpg; p. 10 Kansas City Star/Getty Images; p. 11 Corepics VOF/Shutterstock.com; p. 13 Boston Globe/Getty Images; p. 15 (both) Brian A. Westerholt/Getty Images; p. 17 Pascal Le Segretain/Getty Images; p. 19 (top) Daniel Garcia/Getty Images; p. 19 (bottom) LatinContent/STR/Getty Images; p. 21 (top) Al Bello/Getty Images; p. 21 (bottom) B Bennett/Getty Images.

Cataloging-in-Publication Data

Names: Anthony, David.
Title: Girls play field hockey / David Anthony.
Description: New York : PowerKids Press, 2017. | Series: Girls join the team | Includes index.
Identifiers: ISBN 9781499420975 (pbk.) | ISBN 9781499420999 (library bound) | ISBN 9781499420982 (6 pack)
Subjects: LCSH: Field hockey–Juvenile literature.
Classification: LCC GV1017.H7 A548 2017 | DDC 796.355–d23

# CONTENTS

# DIFFERENT KINDS OF HOCKEY

Hockey is a popular sport played by people all over the world. There are many different versions, or kinds, of hockey. It's easy to figure out where ice hockey is played—on ice! Another kind of hockey is field hockey.

Field hockey is a game played with a stick and a ball. It's most often played on grass or man-made **turf**. In the United States, field hockey is played mainly by girls and women in high school and college. Playing field hockey is a great way to learn skills such as teamwork while having fun outside with your friends!

## Overtime!

While field hockey is mainly a women's sport in the United States, it's played by both men and women in equal numbers in other parts of the world.

Field hockey is just called "hockey" in most countries. However, its full name is most often used in the United States and Canada because of the popularity of ice hockey in those countries.

# AN ANCIENT SPORT

Field hockey has been around for thousands of years! It's believed people in ancient Egypt might have played a kind of field hockey. Other versions were played by the ancient Romans and the ancient Aztec people who lived in what's now Mexico. In the mid-1800s, field hockey became very popular in England. The Hockey Association in London was founded in 1886, and this group made a set of basic rules for the sport.

Until the late 1800s, only men were allowed to play field hockey. The first women's field hockey club was founded in 1887. After that, women's field hockey began to grow in popularity.

## Overtime!

In 1927, the International Federation of Women's Hockey Associations was created. This organization helped field hockey become a sport played by women around the world.

Constance Applebee introduced field hockey to women in the United States in 1901. While studying in the United States, Constance, who grew up in England, showed women at Harvard University how to play the sport. After that, field hockey was played by women at other U.S. colleges.

**Constance Applebee**

**stone carving of field hockey from ancient Greece**

# THE RULES OF THE GAME

Field hockey players score points by shooting the ball into the other team's goal using their stick. Each goal in field hockey is worth one point. Goals can only be scored from inside the part of the field called the shooting circle or striking circle. If a shot is taken from outside the circle, the ball must touch another player in the circle before going in the goal to score a point.

Field hockey players can't use their feet to score or to move the ball down the field. Using small taps of the stick to move the ball down the field is called dribbling.

## Overtime!

Field hockey games are also called matches. A field hockey match is most often broken into two halves that are each 35 minutes long.

The field where field hockey is played is 100 yards (91.4 m) long and 60 yards (54.9 wide. Players have to be in good shape to r up and down such a long field!

goal    shooting circle

100 yards (91.4 m)

60 yards (54.9 m)

# EACH PLAYER'S JOB

Each field hockey team must have 11 players on the field at one time. Teams are made up of offensive players, midfielders, defensive players, and a goalkeeper. Offensive players are called forwards, and defensive players are also known as fullbacks.

A forward's job is to score goals, while a fullback's job is to stop the other team's forwards from scoring. A midfielder plays both offense and defense. This means she helps her team score and helps stop the other team from scoring. A goalkeeper's job is to stop the ball from going in the goal. She gets to use her feet and other body parts that the rest of the players can't use.

goalkeeper

Field hockey players can pass the ball to each other by pushing it with their stick. Fullbacks try to break up these passes to give their team the ball.

## Overtime!

Midfielders must be able to run all over the field to play both offense and defense. They run more than any other kind of field hockey player.

# GEAR FOR THE GAME

If you want to play field hockey, all you really need is a ball and a stick. A field hockey stick is shaped like the letter "J," and it has a rounded side and a flat side. Players use the flat side to move the ball.

Although the ball used to play field hockey is small, it can be hit at the goal with enough power to hurt a goalkeeper. That's why goalkeepers wear special safety **equipment**. This gear includes a helmet, a chest **protector**, and pads for different parts of their arms and legs.

## Overtime!

A field hockey ball can be shot with so much power that it travels up to 100 miles (161 km) per hour!

## goggles

★ protect the eyes

## mouth guard

★ protects the teeth and the rest of the mouth

# FIELD HOCKEY SAFETY EQUIPMENT

## shin guards

★ protect the lower legs and ankles and are often worn with high socks over them

## shoes (cleats)

★ help players run safely on the field

These are the basic pieces of safety equipment worn by field hockey players. Some defensive players also wear masks to protect their face at certain times.

# COLLEGE AND BEYOND

If you work hard on the field and in the classroom, you could play field hockey in college. The **National Collegiate Athletic Association** (NCAA) holds a tournament, or set of games, every year to **determine** the best college field hockey team in the United States.

The best field hockey players in the world face each other every four years in the Hockey World Cup. The first Women's World Cup was played in 1974. While the United States takes part in the Women's World Cup, it's never won this tournament. As of 2014, the only countries that have won the Women's World Cup are Germany, Australia, Argentina, and the Netherlands.

## Overtime!

The NCAA field hockey tournament began in 1981, and it's only for women's teams. There's no men's NCAA field hockey tournament.

Old Dominion University holds the record for the most NCAA field hockey **championships**. As of 2015, this school has won nine championships. The University of Maryland's field hockey team, shown here, is a close second with eight championships.

# AT THE OLYMPICS

Field hockey is a popular sport at the Summer Olympics, which are also held every four years. Like the World Cup, the Olympics feature the world's best field hockey players. The first time field hockey was introduced as an Olympic sport was 1908, but that was only men's field hockey.

Women's field hockey became part of the Olympics in 1980. The U.S. women's field hockey team won a bronze **medal** at the 1984 Olympics, which were held in Los Angeles, California. USA Field Hockey runs camps and other programs you can take part in if you want to play in the Olympics one day!

## Overtime!

In 2014, the 1984 Olympic field hockey team was **inducted** into the USA Field Hockey Hall of Fame.

Kate Middleton

During the 2012 Summer Olympics in London, England, Kate Middleton, the Duchess of Cambridge, was often seen supporting the British women's field hockey team. Kate played field hockey while she was in school before becoming a member of the British royal family.

# "THE MAGICIAN"

Luciana Aymar is considered one of the best female field hockey players of all time. She was born in Argentina, and she became the youngest member ever of that country's national field hockey team. Luciana won four Olympic medals, and she also won four Hockey World Cup medals. She's the only player to win the International Hockey Federation Player of the Year **award** eight times.

In 2015, Luciana was chosen to be an **ambassador** for the 2018 Youth Olympic Games in Argentina. She wants to grow the sport in her home country by helping young people learn to play field hockey.

## Overtime!

Luciana Aymar stopped playing for Argentina's national field hockey team in 2014. She scored 162 goals while playing for her country

**Luciana Aymar**

Luciana Aymar was so good at field hockey that her nickname was "The Magician."

# INDOORS AND ON ICE

Field hockey can also be played inside. Indoor field hockey, or indoor hockey, is very similar to outdoor field hockey, but it's played by teams of six on an indoor field. A U.S. national team plays indoor field hockey matches around the world.

If these versions of hockey sound fun to you, ice hockey might also be a sport you'd like to play. Like indoor field hockey, ice hockey features teams of six players. These players try to get a puck into the other team's goal while skating on ice. This sport is growing in the United States, and many communities have ice hockey teams for girls.

## Overtime!

The National Women's Hockey **League** is a **professional** ice hockey league for women in the United States. It started in 2015.

Women's ice hockey became an Olympic sport in 1998. That year, the United States took home the gold medal. Since then, the U.S. team has won three silver medals and one bronze medal.

# LEARNING ON THE FIELD

You can play hockey inside or outside, on ice or on an outdoor field. No matter where you play it, this sport teaches the value of hard work and **cooperation**. It also teaches you how much fun it is to get moving and be active.

Field hockey is the most popular version of hockey played around the world. It's been around for centuries in different forms, and women have been playing this sport for more than 100 years. Today, girls and women still enjoy playing field hockey—whether it's on a school field or Olympic turf!

# GLOSSARY

**ambassador:** An official messenger or representative.

**award:** A prize given for doing something well.

**championship:** A contest to find out who's the best player or team in a sport.

**cooperation:** The act of working with others to get something done.

**determine:** To officially decide something.

**equipment:** Supplies or tools needed for a certain purpose.

**induct:** To officially make a person a member of a group or organization.

**league:** A group of teams that play the same sport and compete against each other.

**medal:** A flat, small piece of metal with art or words that's used as an honor or reward.

**National Collegiate Athletic Association:** The organization that governs college sports in the United States.

**professional:** Having to do with a job someone does for a living.

**protector:** Something that keeps someone or something safe.

**turf:** The upper layer of soil that is a thick mat of grass and plant roots.

# INDEX

# WEBSITES

Due to the changing nature of Internet links, PowerKids Press has developed
an online list of websites related to the subject of this book. This site is
updated regularly. Please use this link to access the list:
www.powerkidslinks.com/gjt/fhoc